Revelations
Conjuring In Heaven

Front Cover
'Power Struggle'
Lino print
32.2 x 31.3
by Graham Peter Metson

Revelations
Conjuring In Heaven

By

Graham Peter Metson

FORWARD

I have travelled with my imagination into the concept world of the string universe and considered the parallel universes derived from the quantum theories, these images combined with the meditations of complete silence until the sounds, then songs, of the ancient birds vibrated the strings of the void and elegantly moved the electric energy particles of time creating a great harmonious chord of life to be struck, and Heaven on Earth begun. A continuous celebration of life in all its forms of wonder, contradictions and variations of beauty opened towards a future of understanding the joy of knowledge – and, again forward, towards the state of reverence for the tree of knowledge and the tree of life, so that the birds of the universe now sit upon its branches and sing like angels. The branches and songs spiral into infinity and dance with the eternal light and mysterious depths of existence. And all this can be enjoyed by everyman for it is the gift of life. The start of the New Golden Age.

A PERSONAL RESPONSE

Like all my favourite poetry, Graham's verses are burgeoning with big ideas yet restrained in their words. If the description in "An Explanation of Creation" is anything to go by, his mind is an exciting place to be! In this collection he encompasses lines on creation, black holes, Greek mythology, climate change, Biblical imagery, art, the pleasures of whiskey, a Madonna concert, and more personal themes, too.

The synthesis of different ideas in new and interesting ways is a mark of true creativity and in this the reader of Graham's poems is amply rewarded. A favourite of mine is "I No Longer Believe the Weatherman" which moves from the unreliability of weather reporting to a comment on "the climate of love". The contrast between "hell ... descending on dark fast wings" and the "angel on a star/A heart on fire" is beautifully pointed, again using a few, well chosen words.

Some synthesis borders on paradox and so encourages the reader to think. Mixed metaphors used to be frowned on, but here they flourish in free abandon, pushing out the limits of imagination. Read "God of Silence" and expect to be both thrilled and perplexed. "A silence so deep, it supports architecture" becomes in turn a "deep pool", "a fortress in a cliff", "a vibrant invisible web" and a finally "a wedge between the worlds". Each image is fertile and promising; together they form a rich garden of various scents and colours.

A surprising comparison presents itself to us in the rapid-fire and rollicking lines on "Titian". Whether consciously or not, Graham has described his poetic vision for us in his tribute to the visual artist. The poet, too, is a "magician ... wonder was his mission". His best poems, like a Titian canvas, have "no need for any addition", combining "oranges, reds, greens, yellow, clashing". The addition of this last word reminds us what no poet can avoid: some of their lines are bound to rub us up the wrong way.

However, it is perhaps as a musician of words that Graham can best be understood. He captures the echoes of an ancient song and, rephrasing them in modern terms, delights us with the endless variations that are possible. As he says in "The Deep Dream Song":

> *I lift my guitar*
> *And strum*
> *The deep dream song*
> *For everyone.*

If you are a fellow dreamer, then dream on: you will find yourself enthralled!

Dr. Paul Martin

CONTENTS

Poetry Portraits – 16 Selected Poems

God Of Silence

Silence.
Before the chorus at dawn.
Silence, of the setting sun
Therapeutic thermals of calm
Shimmering with negative power.

A silence so deep, it supports architecture
Cementing the bricks of dreams.
Meditate, create in this deep pool
Of silent solitude
Internal walls of silence
Sliced out of the twenty-first century
Like a fortress in a cliff.

This meaningful silence is like prayer
Religious in its magnitude
Stretching from this centre
To the edges of the universe
A vibrant invisible web
Woven by the God of Silence
As mystical as the creative powers
It drives a wedge between the worlds.

Revelation

The winds of the world have passed over me.
Now I sit in England, meditating
On which future direction
I should take.

Watching the Whore of Babylon devour
The treasures of life
And in turn she will be devoured
By the monsters of her own beckoning.

Then there will be a natural order
Of reverence for life
And for all the elements of the Earth.

Finally, the search for the love of Heaven.

The Living Jewel

When the light strikes right across the bay
The rainbow arches the clean blue sky
As the pure water runs through your hands
You view the vast pleasures of the land.

The world lovingly has the moon in tow
As the shooting stars shoot, firing the night
Emotions move from stop to go.
Doesn't it just make you feel right?
Isn't it good to be here today?
So great to be alive
On this living jewel
Floating past the Milky Way.

Protected by our atmosphere –
It's safe to dream
Feel real, surreal
The evening beautiful and so clear
Doesn't it just make you want to
Stand up and cheer?

The Deep Dream Song, (The Song Of The Birds)

Sung by the ancient birds
The sound verse
Created the universe.

Songs within songs
Life within life
Ring, rhythm and rhyme
Through layers of time.

The deep dream song
Is yours and mine.
Everyone, everything,
Forever and always
For better, for worse
Let us all sing
The sacred verse.

I lift my guitar
And strum
The deep dream song
For everyone.

Where To Now?

Living in the light
Growing
Experience the bright,
Active light
Open to its life
Standing upright
Enjoy the good light
Absorbing the force
Seeing silence
Hear the light sounds
Listen to the light words pound
Upon the crumbling rust
Light particles of daylight dust.
The climate changes weathers
Reality is running out, for us
(Here today, gone tomorrow)
At the speed of light.

References To Wisdom

Angelica holds the reins of the dragon
The dragon content by her side
St George blindly stabs the dragon
He being always the true beast
Angelica looks silently down
Handing the reins to the knight

The Holy Church of Rome
Complained of Michelangelo's lack of progress
Forced from his sick bed
Michelangelo resumed his task
With stabbing cold and gagging cough
Suspended on high
Casting his eye over the Sistine Chapel.
Below the Pope's attire became unconvincing
In act and deed which was nearest to Heaven.

The Tree of Life
Remained unfunded. The people
Complained the money could be better spent
Politicians heeded the majority
Creativity withered with starvation
The sick did not recover, the poor remained content
Wisdom died its spirit spent.

(Note: The first verse is a cross reference combining two
similar mythical stories or tales that of Roger and Angelica
and St George and the dragon.)

Abstract

Orange singing in the rain
Crystal eyes that explain
Passions that fan the flame.
Shapes that drive you insane
Sounds from Heaven
Things you can't explain.

Abstract for change
Everything is re-arranged
Feeling safe but strange
Mysterious waters ripple
Communication exchange
(Impressions left on the senses)

Speaking with silence
Stations of experience
Fingers in the tangled mane
Blurring the frames
Breaking of logic
Two colours plead
Understanding a need.

The true path of the heart, freed
Energy gathering speed.
A journey untamed
Alchemy tantalisingly unexplained.

The Chimera Secret

We the human race
With our knowledge and wisdom
Will create the Chimera
With fusion and cross-breeding
Of species and particles of energy.

The magnificent Chimera
Race of guardians
Will traverse the universe and heavens
Carrying in their 'boxes' our history and deeds.

The Chimera will sing our 'songs'
In the silence of the void
After all has changed and perished
Until the new calling
Begins the cycle again.

A Quarter-Past-Ever

Nature is overtaking Death
In the form of modern man
It's a quarter-past-ever
Now we are holding back the dam
Controlling the gate of time
Forever everything will be sublime.

It's a quarter-past-Heaven
In the history of man
As we transform into angels
The millennium is harking
The coming again
Sound the trumpets of light
And pray the calculation is right.

It's a quarter-past-ever
Forever
Cancel the concept of never.

Horses Of War And Peace

Pegasus winged above Medusa
Troy wooden with inner human life
Silent before the alarm

The Parthenon frieze stolen from the temple
Remains a timeless token treasure
Triumph transforms truth
An illegal stain on British Art
Forbidden their place of origin
Horses of Aphrodite Apollo and Zeus
Apocalypsed nightmares of conquest
Unleash the beasts of war

Dangerous but gentle herds and breeds
Measured by hand
Those that have charged in battle
Stand smouldering sculpture still
Shire horses that pull the plough
Pinned with competition colours

In England
Myth and legend the horned unicorn
Beneath the shaded green bough
Invisible now.

Conjured by culture
Prehistoric minds forced to elegance
Raced at the Derby
For the amusement of modern mankind
Breaking their spirit
To make an easy dime.

Friend

It's so good to have a friend
Send your dreams
Explain what life means
To a friend

Keep them in mind
Spend all our time
Be there, from the start to the very end
Care, share all you can, help a friend

Extend a hand
Open your heart
Need, bleed, worry frantic
Tear yourself apart
For a friend

Rage, be extreme
Be forgiven, redeemed
Act your worst
Deservedly cursed.
Understood, by a friend

Lift them up high
Reach for the sky
Send up a balloon
Fly to the moon!
With a friend.

Be at peace with a friend.

The Great Storm

Gravity churned at the tide
The Devil sat in his chariot. Ride
Mighty Zeus and Ra on either side
Their power opened the skies
Weather created to take lives
Composed from spells and foreboding tragic
A great horizontal mass of magic
Smashed the edge of the land
At the Devil's command
All life was damned
Witchcraft scarred the Earth
Drowning the spirits of joy and mirth
Man swept aside by Jupiter's curse.

Titian

We all love Titian
He is a magician
Colour and tradition
Wonder was his mission
Everything in perfect position
No need for any addition
The human condition
With God's permission
The naked truth
The pagan's hoof
Angels aloof
Saints, beauty and passion
Depicted in a sacred fashion
The bacchanal party crashing
Landscape and blue nature
(Robes of strong silk colours)
Orange, reds, greens, yellow, clashing
Absolutely smashing!

An Explanation Of Creation

So that's how it happens

Like a volcano the ideas
Seething to the top exploding
Around my head flying
Fragmenting, some
Surviving
Others overheated
Gushing, like geysers
In this chaos melt down
Things gel together
Disconnected thoughts join and make sense

An idea
A whole thing just lives
Suspended
Like atoms in a vacuum
Glowing in a void
(Between nature, reason and imagination)
Where time and creative thoughts meet

Ideas boxed grow wings and speed
Between time zones like visual Mozart.

I No Longer Believe The Weatherman

He told us to expect minus eight winds
That hell was descending on dark fast wings
But look, the sun is shining through
The sky is radiant blue
A sign from nature
That is honest and true.

An angel on a star
A heart on fire –
A naked woman dancing in its flame
The climate of love left unexplained
I'll never believe the weatherman again.

No
I no longer believe the weatherman
The confusion he brings!
May he be forgiven for his sins.

Goddess Madonna

With the moon crossing above
Eighty thousand stare
In wonderment and love
As you take the stage
Electronic trumpets and rhythms flare
The night sky tremors
Because you're standing there
Cult goddess, queen, so fair.

The audiences' energy is absorbed
Reflected in turn with creative rewards
The fans now in a magical trance
Entwined in artistry and dance
Transforming the local environment
From hill land to the heavens above
A tribute to your poetry and art
You stir our minds and our hearts.

Dancing to the beat, all action and heat.
Simultaneously presenting your desires
The music transpires
A population meaningfully inspired
The 'confessions' complete
Your message transcends all barriers
Your image magnified and multiplied
To goddess like stature
You leave the crowd in raptures.

Afterwards
Well meaning gestures are waved
Deserved compliments are made
Guardians are offered for your protection
And praise
To the goddess Madonna, we all crave.

When tortured countries required
A woman of the world
You went, and gave them irrespective
A New Yorker's perspective
Then with a final graceful twirl
Returned to England
Where you are loved like a royal pearl
For being that 'model' American 'girl'
Abraham Lincoln would have respected you
Just for being you.

Eighty thousands lights say adieu
Goddess Madonna, *whew!*

Falling

In England the leaves are turning golden brown
And falling, falling
Your beautiful towers are twisting
Lovers are falling, falling
We want to put our arms around you.
To put our arms out to save you.
Flight path, flight path, flight path
Passenger prisoners smash
The building walls agape
Twisted metal arrows, shattered dreams.

A blast of hate the centre is falling
It's all too appalling!
A massacre of innocence
All our passion, tears and love
All our prayers unanswered.

The dust is settling on the flowers
Petals falling, falling
America in mourning, dreams are falling
Eros, far too late (tears are falling)
Give thanks for those who did escape.

Comment

Soon we won't be able to breathe
Or watch the change of the seasons
Nor admire the colours of the leaves.

The present is obliterating history
To accommodate the future.

The painters have been persecuted
The musicians muted
The poets polluted
Life diluted
Our dreams looted!

Let's put a congestion charge on love
Now wouldn't that be super.

Tomorrow, society will ration passion
Well, it is rather out of fashion.

Disappearing

(Scotland) A beautiful mathematical equation
Explains the evasive evaporation
Of our disappearing universe.

Like a magical play
Its visual twist
Of segments missed
Reality slipping away.

That 'turning' day
The thin fin man
Like a human fish
Disappeared into the Scottish mist.

That strange night
Skies full of balloons and ancient bliss
Of fragile flying machines
(A Jules Verne vision)
Historical images of flight
Modernism absent from sight.

A stroking of the chin –
Disturbing this disappearing thing.

(England)

First, just small things
People getting out of half -cars
Their legs cease to exist
Dissected by thin air. And
Time and space
Unable to resist
The universal shift.

A crowd of men suddenly appear
Talking, chatting heartily
Then no more
The pavement empty and clear.
Everything out of gear.

A black hole is eating somewhere near
Swallowing our universe like a good beer.

From the platform at the station
Semi-transparent apparitions
Glide silently by. Poltergeists
From a parallel universe, mysteriously queer
Mechanical ghosts
Never stopping here.

In the park a seated Buddha figure
Slipping away, silently slipping away
Shimmers slowly and is no more
Gone as if through an invisible door.

Need I say more?

(Thanks to Professor Stephen Hawking)

Celebration Child

(The Miracle Poem)

As the child reaches for her hand
That moment, it feels its mother's love
That touch we all understand
As a blessing from Heaven above.

We see the celebration child
A spirit running wild.
A peaceful, sleeping dream
Toys, games and delights
Discovery of a mind and soul
A future strong and bold
A beauty to behold.

In the bright newborn eyes
A life stretches out
Enriching our thoughts. This prize
Without a doubt
The perfect gift of hope.

A life as bright as the flowers
Bathed in love
The joy of all your hours
Celebration child
Your true name will be ours.

Jaguar

The owner of a Jaguar
Walks with a swagger
Metallic dream machine
Moves like a silver dagger.

Engineered acceleration
Causes transformation
Machine-man combination
A design celebration.

Spiralling gears
Advanced ideas
Interior veneers
Luxury leather
Marble dashboard
Perfection award
Beauty restored.

Party On The Moon

Let's have a party on the moon
With moon maidens with balloons
Inscribed with slogans such as
'Come up to my room on the moon
Please make love to me soon
At the party on the moon.'

With jelly suspended above my spoon
Dancing weightless, not marooned
Leave your worldly worries behind
I invite the whole world to –
The party on the moon.

Imagine making love on the moon
Free and fluid, floating in a dream
Can you just see what I mean?
Let's have that party on the moon
Like a party you have never seen
Let's have the cats' whiskers cream
Everybody laughing on the moon.

Across the moonscape we will fly
Space fireworks, illuminating the universal sky
With streamers, champagne and wine
Having a great time
Listen to that moon music
I'm sure we will all be in tune
At the party on the moon
There's plenty of room!

Let's do it soon
Have a party on the moon
Hopefully angels from Heaven
Will join us soon
At the party on the moon.
Forever having fun
We'll chase away the gloom
Oh party on the moon.

No Time

The drifters are camped out on the range
Enjoying an evening meal.
The trail boss is deeply concerned, 'Look . . .'
Exchanging whispered words with the cook.

Ranch hands are swapping dreams
Strangers drop in
With fresh water from the stream
Sharing their supplies
(One traveller sounds profoundly wise)

So, in no time
Everyone is getting along just fine.

The trail boss is taken by surprise
As cow girls on speckled ponies arrive
These women wear coloured ribbons
And have rainbow sparkling eyes
They offer tankards of amber nectar and Firewater brew
Everybody is saying, 'How do you do.'

'There's no way of stopping it now,' exclaims the cook
'That would be a crime
Everyone will have to be allowed
To have a damn good time!'

The Visit

What's that rippling in the chair
Is there somebody invisibly there
Or is it just the breeze?
My intense stare
Or lonely despair
Is there something, somebody really there?
Moving like a current of air
That moves the seat cover and leaves the armchair
For that long moment the unknown mystery
And the seventh dimension exists
Felt by my electric hair.
I declare, I'm sure a presence was there
As my awareness tunes and flares
With the music of existence, movement, time and space
I no longer feel on my own
The company lives not like you or I
Without muscle, marrow jelly or bone
On a level of its own.
Perhaps on its journey home it stopped to observe an inferior being
Just for amusement, or to take in something lost long ago
Its substance
It or I no longer know
As we appreciate life's afterglow.
Let's take account of things to date
Better do it now or it may soon be too late
While the life-force generates
Before I lose the right to elegantly escape
From this supernatural puzzle
Let's just file this experience under interesting event to debate.
Put on the television and have a large slice

Of Christmas birthday cake
For goodness sake
It was surely only a trick of the eye
Or what other people call
Pie in the sky!

The Visitors

It is burning. Dry
Arid
Far too hot for England.
The visitors have come
To milk us again
For we are like cows to them
Also discreetly just
To look, to tame
They are looking at you

They become us
Our energy they seep and sap
Live off our backs
We carry them invisibly about
Inside and out

Like royalty, or military
During their planetary invasion
The conquerors sleep with us
In a hidden way
Bird-faced, ant-headed
Insect legs, cat like
Winged shadow, sly
They can be the spider, symbolically
We the fly
(Mutation of transformation)
Eagle or fox
Nature masks them. These
Metamorphic hosts, honorary ghosts.

If you can see in the night –
There:
One luminous figure, slumbering
On my shoulder
Outlined in light
The other –
Cheekily, awake and dangerous
Reclining, illuminated cat like
Its whole body a mischievous grin
Strikes at my awareness
They are there alright.

The visitors – semi transparent
Flickering forms
Shadows
Fleeting, something obscured
Behind a screen, glanced
Like a dream,
They would have you believe
But real, sensed
Annoyingly unseen.

Blanched transport, invisible
To the normal eye –
But search for a false star
One that should not be
Below their cosmic
Camouflaged craft
Suspended in our sky.
Hear a clicking
At the back of your head
A sting on your back
Like a needle point
The room turns in and black

A groaning in your limbs
Perspiration on the brow, cold
A melting in the brain
If they are displeased
They attempt to drive you insane
For your sins
For your previous sins
A stigmatization of rays
The last supper delayed

As a reward you may get
Like a gift to a pet
Their developed third eye –
To the time tunnel
Down you go
They and we are all
In there
For they are us
From now to here
Silence is all
That you will hear
A brush past you
Like a light breeze
If you're not perfect
They will leave

These policeman from another day
Like actors their appearance change
Can multiply and clone
The same but different surface array

The visitors control the heat
Of the day
It is cool and wet with rain
They have left
And gone on their way

Their 'prisoners' remain
In a jaded way
With red, burning, irritating skin
Wondering
When will they return to 'play'
Who will they use
Or take away
I strongly advise, imply and condone
Don't let them wear you down to the bone
The safest thing to do
Is to stay at home
If you wish to remain the same
Human by name

You will all know now
The signs, be ready
When the visitors call again

My coffee is cold
Give thanks, more rain.

Gulliver's Well-Mannered Friends

Gulliver quite rightly
Had great respect for the horse
Thinking it higher in hygiene
Intellect and morals
More so than the common man
They were not mythical nor magical
Just better at conversation and discourse
And didn't seem to smell so bad
His obsession with them
Drove his wife quite mad.

(With thanks to Jonathan Swift)

My Guitar

She took hold of my hand
And just melted
Like curtains of dappled light
Shimmering out of sight
The rhythm of the day
Passed behind us
The moments mounted
We were exalted
Minds and doors opened
Our shadows became sculptures
Daylight flooded in
As barriers were broken
Everything was given and taken

When the moon rotated
Natural time suspended
Our feelings blended
To nature we surrendered
By the evening mood befriended
Touch and memory
Fired to splendour
Love shook us through the night.

On Mother's Side

Grandfather was Irish through and through from Waterford
Mr Murray spelt with an 'a', called Dad by all members of the
family
Educated out of school with the fishing line and rod
Preserving and promoting the culture of the building site
With a flutter on the horses to keep hope alight
He kept chickens in his council house garden shed
When it took his fancy a chicken he would behead.

Wearing bicycle clips, a Woodbine legend
A pocket watch that never told a lie and a feathered stalking
hat
He could be seen regularly outside the betting shop
Where he'd greet you with a nod
For country crafts he had quite a knack
He picked watercress from the rivers and ground raw
horseradish
To make an extra 'bob'
Inside the house sat by the fire sucking on a length of straw
His opinion was up for grabs and going for a song
With the occasional mutter he would make a request
Otherwise content just to rest.

Old Scottish Whisky

Old Scottish whisky
It's simply the best
The quick way to Heaven
Because it is blessed

A whole bottle!
If you need a good rest
Malt, Glenmorangie, a liquid caress
Spirit of the grain; matured to drive you insane
Guaranteed to set fire
To your brain

Full to the hilt (just a wee dram)
If you need a jilt
Give the glass a tilt
You're out in the street

Old Scottish whisky
It's simply the best
The quick way to Heaven
Because it is blessed.

24-hour Domestic Machines

Early morning
Radios talking
Television screen transmission speaking
News, information heaping
Computers thinking, blinking, thinking
Electric fire buzzing
Washing machine moaning
Electric ovens groaning
Microwave bleeping
The old cat keeps sleeping
Electric kettle peaking
My mind is shrieking
Hoovers reaping
Cars are beeping
Security devices attention seeking
Mobile phones repeating
Hot water systems seeping
Wall radiators heating
Machines with us
To the day's completion
Automatically timed company
Through the night creeping
Machine noises are creaking
Restrained telephone clock alarms beating
Will soon be bleating
24-hour domestic machines.

The Seed

As the seed grew in the earth
It thought of the bud to be.
The bud loved the dream
Of the blossomy scent -
That it became it
From this union
Came the berry.

Kitchen Window Eclipse

Ancient ancestral fears
Foretold by the seers
Take care, beware this mystery play
The astral orbs perform today

Pearl grey
Cloud cover, dismay
A daytime dusk fell. Staged
Across the sky – total solar eclipse day
Obscured by coal grey. Lunar powers
Atmospherically adjusted to display
A cool stone liquid curtain

Waiting, waiting – open revealed
A silver sun, watching. Hung
Edged with grey light
Magical moon
Moving through Neptune gray
Moon and sun
Imminent to embrace as one

Subdued orange light. The
Birds stopped in flight
A worldly stillness –
Two minutes like night

Time stopped
Traffic stopped. Silence smoked
Glass, inverted –
Introverted
Primitive insight (The sky a mask)
Primitive instinct. Mind flight

To crouch down, lay flat.
To flee, an intuitive warning
Of that dark craft thaumaturgy
Cast Nature's law
Like a spell

Free now from science
The moon into the sun scored
An old dramatic crossing of sacred paths
A physical séance dance
Pass-over – advanced travellers
Gracefully disengaged from heavenly rapport
The eclipse passed the Earth by
Certain, nothing was left to chance

English skies return at last
Kitchen window returns to glass

Pause (rainbow applause).

(11th August 1999)

Docking Motion

That sound moved towards you
Distant siren
A first awareness of a repeated vision
Mass, volume, precision
Carried by lapping waters
Allowing this miracle of industry
An unexpected grace
Granted by Neptune
The lightness of a hovercraft
Massive, floating merchant
Metal and men at last
Sliced through the permitted entrance
I watched in a trance

Docking in silence
As if a giant slow falling rock
Came concisely to rest
Finding its place
It anchored at the dock

At night-lit-self illuminating
Against the dark Scottish skyline
That this practical vessel
Could convey such art
One could only have an admiration
For the everyday, for everyman

Then to relive the wonder
When again
It did depart.

Love Is . . .

Love is . . .
The moon in your hair
The sun in June
Morning fresh dew
Love is you
Love is saying hello
Love is saying, 'Don't go'

Love is . . .
Enjoying the rain
The pure light of the day
The rainbow after the storm
Dancers moving with grace
Like that beautiful smile
On your elegant face

Love is . . .
Picasso's dove
The stars up above
The bird on the wing
When the choirs sing

Love is
The rhythm of the band
Love is . . .
Lending a hand
The heavenly piano and violin
Love is when the saxophone makes it swing

Love is working hard
Love is getting it right
Love is not giving up
Love is standing your ground
Love is . . .
Laughing out loud
Making everyone feel easy
Being strong not giving in
Love is the opposite to sin

Love is just being here
Love is living
Love is giving
Love is forgiving
Love is being free without fear.

For Future Children

A Poetic Introduction to the Time Travellers Manual
(Model AETM Mark II)

I have to say
That I have read many poems
About time travel in my day
But none explain it particularly well
Take it from a true and experienced
Time traveller pioneer
That often it can be literally sheer hell
As you read on hopefully you will agree
That it is just as well
Or should I say swell
That I do not have an AETM Mark II
Time machine to sell

First you step into the machine
Switch on, and you're gone
The journey starts off quiet enough
Sitting, standing, floating and eventually body bloating
In the flight control chamber
At frightening stationary light speed
There is really nothing else that you need
To feel so fantastic at full stationary light speed
As you eclipse yourself every light second
There's nothing can touch it for glee
Take it as gospel from me.

But then everything implodes and you turn inside out
And follow your life like tea poured out of a spout
Splitting into particles or so it seems
You are no longer substance only substance of dreams
Your whole being is converted into a glowing light beam
But your eyes remain still while you're rotating at 360 degrees
A tremendous flood of information enters your brain
And you know you will never be the same again.

Rotating, escalating at stationary light speed
Your whole body feels pushed down into your semi-transparent knees
With a fantastic rush of adrenaline you suddenly feel extremely pleased
Then abhorrently quite ill
As your life's experiences flash back images shudder, then freeze
Including memories of people, events, hopes, triumphs and disease
All stacked back on the shelfs in your mind
(All in order if, or as you please)
Then add to this a temporary sensation of going quite blind
While everything appears to multiply by nine.

A new bright space created before you opens and appears
Quickly filled in with your newly acquired wisdom and fears
The journey U turns it shoots passed your extracted right ear
Now coming to a close
As your five right toes
Neatly attach themselves to your nose.

Just as you start to relax you discover that
Your left foot is stuck and your sense of smell
Is retreating round a bend
In a time warp blend
Simultaneously your DNA decides to distort
You whole life rushes past you
This could be the end your senses report.

The winged messenger Mercury then mercifully happens by
And gives you an enormous shove
You feel you're gong to die
As everything quickly falls back into place
And you take your rightful place again
In your own time and space.

As for your time journey there is not a visible trace
Except that your forehead pulses
And your body has obtained a state of grace
These rewarding prize symptoms as described above
Depends on the quality of the person and
Their ability to absorb intelligence and love
And is therefore not always the guaranteed case
To be able to achieve such an exalted final state.

After such a journey I hasten to add
The major problem is not just indigestion
And suffering from time lag
But what a boring time everybody else has had
In comparison to you perpetually feeling inwardly glad
At having obtained all that universal knowledge, by gad
Now that can't be bad.

But on the surface you will look continually sad
It's that mystery of contradiction
That all the time travellers have
A combination of illness, good fortune and power.

Finally please do remember to clean
And service your time machine
Particularly this one
That runs like a dream
If you want to buy one
You'll understand why
I am not particularly keen
To arrange such a deal
Nor encourage a mutual business scheme
Because then I would no longer be
The time traveller, artist, poet supreme.

Moth Connections

The moon in June
Stalks the bee hawks winged walk
Jaunty tiger in a spot
The thin purple line
Sable brush stroke so fine
Cinnabar coasting
Captures gypsies with
Black arch movements
Blossom kinetic flower
Emerald peach with
Peppered tail
Collides with puss
Hawks mother of pearl
Hunts the foxglove
With stained glass lace wings
A song of desire.

Red Admiral

Red admiral coming aboard
Silent floating mobile
Scuppers the decks of the garden boarders
Flutters its colours like blown dandelions
Pied Piper movements
Red flight – green lawn
Butterfly gliding
Optical device of contrasting and complimentary colour and
form
Keel hauls the pansies
One follows it journey from prow to aft
Disappearing into foliage
In search of a crow nest
In nature's mast
Flickering its medals
Land ho!
Coming to rest at last
Exhausted by its sea shanty dance.

Summer Conversation

The sun plunged out of the sea
The air caressed the land
In the distance space
Music filtered the sky with melody
The earth absorbed the heat
And breathed out again with life
Then the evening fresh with night
The darkness slowly succumbed to the moonlight.

My Stomach Loves Christmas

The Yorkshire pudding follows the turkey
Brussel sprouts by the pound
Oh I can feel it going down
The taste it is tremendous
The world is warmly rotating round
Oh my stomach just loves Christmas
My feet are off the ground

The crispy edged parsnips
Wrapped in cranberry sauce
So enjoying the first course
My taste buds are ringing
My body is singing
Dreaming of dessert
God bless this roasted potato
Resting in my stomach today
It has such a flavour
Cooked by angels I would say
Cooked by angels I would say
I can feel it going down
The stuffing like a scented gown
Nestles with the chicken breasts
A honeyed golden brown
Oh my stomach loves Christmas
I can feel it going down

Cauliflower, cauliflower,

Cauli flower

I can feel it going down
The stuffing like a scented gown
Nestles with the chicken breasts
A honeyed golden brown
Oh my stomach loves Christmas
I can feel it going down!
I'm in utopia's realm
So let's have another round.

(Can be sung in a jubilant celebration manner)

Anthropology

Poem code note (F) = 'invisible text' for readers' information/instruction only.

The poem reads from left to right with internal central movements indicated by text placements that could be communicated by a change of voice tone or vocal movement, especially if related to a sound recording of this work. If text is in extra large print form then special emphasis in volume should be given to such a particular word or letter.
Anthropology is a minimal word play poem.

∞ - mathematical code for infinity. < = is less than. > = is greater than.

Skin derma		skeleton	blood
	AND		
Mind	(F: word chant x 2)		soul
Bone			muscles
Skull			marrow
		Sen-sori-um	
Mouth			organs
Speak			hair
Tension	brain		patterns
	Lungs smoke		
Tendons			pulse

               H20   94%
               Solid / liquid substances

Sweat   teeth
Eat   sweet
Meat   rib

               Cage –
               Heart

Desires   dreams

               Spine rotates
               Groin
Manipulates   Water   <bowel>   movements

               Birth
               Breaks
Joints   encase   hands
Fingers   point

               (Oracle speaks)

Smell   moods
Sight   moves
Sounds   crowd
Touch   beauty
Hear   sensory   thoughts
Feel   history

               THAUMATURGY IS POSSIBLE
Tough   tender   creed
Nuclear(Family traits)   Gender   mates
Veins   bulge
Acids   feed
Greed   infertility   (Invests)   Infests
Sleep   rests

<u>Lifelines/cross</u>

Psychological   /   frustration
Personal   veneration
Unwanted   explanation
Lacks   imagination?

Man
Wo   Woe
One

Many   alone
Physical   appearances   deleted
Aureole halo
Rele a s e
Spiritual   time   shadow
Venomous addictions cease
Ancients   age
Youth   evolved
Grew   younger
Hunger
For nothing
Passions   fold
Ligaments rolled

ZerO
EmotiOns
Consume   nature
Breathe   death
Invisible

Prognosis:

Love?
Alpha   omega
∞

And When The Calm Came

And when the calm came
And all had gone to sleep
And then awoken again
The land did melt and blend anew
Though man's touch still remained upon it
It was born
Fresh for you.

Still Life With Mackerel

So still. A dream of reality
Through the looking glass
Full brimmed red claret
Colour conjures fragrance
Time trapped liquid mercury
Forever fresh fish
Shining river eye
Silver scaled mackerel
Basked in lemon light
Orange glow responds
To drapery flake white
Fruits fresh with daylight
I drink to your permanence and truth.

Memories Of Making

Influences of the classical mind
Romantic English traditional art
Fuels my contemporary creative flame
The inner me that keeps me sane
Blisters, erupts, sparks and blasts
With haunting mysterious knowledge
Readings of the occult
Feelings of the heart
The secret doctrine
Helps the mind uncoil
And gracefully come apart
A hidden passion to make beauty
Images of angels from Italian Renaissance art
Intertwined with the fury of Van Gogh's darker Dutch
subjects
Then a liking for yellow on both our parts
To his expressive mind blowing French swirls
His individuality and humanity
Like a cloak of many colours
Symbolically enrobes Vincent
The legendary unique iconic pearl
A modern master, an example for us all
Like a being from another world.

So much more opens the door
Shadows of the foundations
The broad framework
From which I start
The seeds of my art
Opposites, contradictions
Ancient Egypt to Robert Rauschenberg
Fusions of old and new

A techno magic of fleeting impressions
From light to dark
An array of lines, textures and marks
So many choices play their part
How the gift of freedom bestows
A double edged sword
A continuous stream of creative thought
Never an opportunity to ever rest or even feel
bored.Scientific, photographed, infra red
Satellite, telescopic visual recordings
Distant galaxies and nebula, dead
Our universe and stars reproduced
And able to be held in my hands
Pictures grasped by our knowledge
Reaped from afar
Segments of infinity, an endless source
Reality and legend bled
Captured and coloured by electric solar power
Suggestions of hell and of heaven
Memories of remorse, the number seven
Landscapes from Scotland to Devon
A personal code of duende
To bind this diverse visual choir
To keep it fresh but mature
Mutually fluid, sharp and obscure.

Politely stolen from Blake, now how
The Ancient of Days oversees
The Chinese belief of the Golden Flower
A one inch Spiritual Square
As universal collected thoughts endow
A circulated heavenly body, a cosmic pear
Between the sun and the moon
Guarded by the dragon of darkness

Treasures of the sacred and profound
Energise a powerful bloom
That requires no earthly nurture
Nor demands infinite room
Created of concepts beyond the norm
Of substances that can not be bought
Compact immaculate glowing form
Magical petals of light and thought
Wise and coded continually sought.

Charcoal, tempera, gouache, watercolour
Acrylic, white pencil, crayon of oil
A remarkable mixed media technique
That rises to the artist's call
On canvas stretched and primed on board
A surface of resonance to which
This work eventually conforms
Dragged by dragon horns to completeness
Ready to be fixed, varnished, glazed and framed
Something new and strange, is born
A twentieth century art form.

Poetry Portraits
16 Selected Poems

Dutch Woman by Van Gogh

Strong face
Full look, serious
Penetrating
Her portrait dominates
The darkness
He appreciates her depth
A noble subject
She has worked hard all her life
The tension of survival
A lived in wisdom
She wonders why –
He struggles to realise her
The white bonnet becomes her
Crown
He has finished.
Now she becomes
Just another potato eater
Returns to her every day
He thanks them all
And moves on
The wildness is yet to come.

Soutine

Soutine knew about paint
He made paintings
With handfuls of loaded brushes

Meagre meals of sumptuous paint
Carcasses of ox drenched with oil
French pastry cooks, hotel workers
Waiters form contemporary icons
White figure, red figure against blue black

Landscapes writhe. Twisting
Tree, earth and sky paint
Reality dissolves, organic structures merge
Encapsulated energy
Fish paint, drying blood
Surfaces of solitude
Memories of Modigliani

Seriously seeking the right place
Harangued by war, politics and ill health
Standing alone on his path
(He claimed success)

A wild dignity of will
To create his art.

Rembrandt Portrait Of The Artist

Old age is so all knowing
So profound
Understanding weakness
But strong
Rembrandt has known the
Lighter and darker sides
Of life, like chiaroscuro
He paints his wisdom
He paints himself for us all to see
The majesty of human life

On his journey
What was it he found?
That look
That silence
These are his gifts to you and me
It gave him meaning
Explains that religious light
Across the brow.

Picasso

Picasso twentieth century
Master
Painter of love, passion,
Horror and disaster
Lean blue years and
Pink circus laughter
Cubist classic innovator
Invented art like a sunburst
(To quench the vultures thirst)

Celebrated creator
Maker of sculptures, prints
Ceramics of nature
Cheered and held in reverence by his people
He plundered El Greco, Greek myth and Africa
Then mixed it with his Spanish blood
Only age forced him to throw down the glove.

Matisse

Art like a good armchair
Colours with a Moorish Moroccan heat
French interiors slumber a dream of summer sleep
The blue of the Mediterranean Sea
Joins company with elegant hotel suites
Red and pink studios
Compositions of earthly idyllic rhythm and Stravinsky beat

Pure line, considered form and print
Convey an intelligence complete
Family, friends, lovers, models, dancers and nymphs
Raise your glass and toast Matisse

For celebrated collages of joy
Chapel white (his spirit speaks)
Like his paintings
Glows with light
Creator of comfort and peace
This civilised family man mandarin
Who was the leader of the 'wild beasts'.

Renoir

Luminous models
Natural and gentle in nature
Reclining
Bathed in impressionist light
Portrayed in sunlight hours
Adorned with jewellery and vivid flowers

Years of knowledge, slight of hand
This craftsmanship could command
A special time and place
The magic of a beautiful face
Contemporary beauty, ancient themes
French landscape scenes
His paintings smiled –
Family life, boating parties and café dances
Homely warm interiors, maternity
Music rooms and river bathers
Silk complexions in sparkling champagne
Reality painted like a dream

Later with aching body and rheumatic hands
His images now recreated as sculpture
Passing on his wisdom
Understanding human and worldly nature
Life's mysteries hold us in a rapture
As we stand before the works of this
Great Master.

Degas L'absinthe Drinkers

A fellow artist and actress
Silent together but not,
Bound by their pastimes
The world filters by

They were just what he wanted
A reflection of his lifestyle
They were like him
Waiting
Washed over by life. Real
Not expecting to be noticed
Stillness attracts attention

They are all three meditating
On life, in their own way
But invisibly touching each
Others worlds. Hazed by alcohol

His impressionistic manner
Suits their tone
He sees their shadows –
They all accept each other.

Monet
The Great Impressionist

Branches of entangled brush strokes
Bridges of petals.
Water of light
The meeting of the elements
Connected by his eye
(What an eye).

Scanned by his sight
The landscape is a sensation
Accepted without verbal explanation
That nature is right
Everything is energy and light
Nature standing draped in
Daylight
Shrouded in French mist.

Elegant figures on the seashore
The promenade erupts like a musical score.
Artists and lovers in boats
Along the Seine are moored
Painting the inlets of the river
Fresh with early morning dew.
The great impressionist Monet
Never faltered from what he loved and knew.

Along the cliffs of erupting sea spray
His entourage of wife, friends and children
Each carry a canvas
For a particular time of the day
As Monet's art moved from dawn to dusk
Until the winter snow changed his view

Staring at the magpie
Painting in the freezing cold morning
Until his hands froze blue.

Then in the cities
Fascinated by their light
How it falls on architecture
Dissolves solids into daylight
Structures shimmer to shadows
As if viewed by a bird in flight.

A return to the garden
The water lilies dance
And conjure a world of delight
His eyes drink France
He feels nature, creates the `Decorations'
Then vision slowly becomes night.

Monet's Japanese bridges
Join two immense cultures
At a stroke
His genius provokes
A world understanding
Reality, art and hope.

Mondrian

Geometrical roots
Pure plastic primary grids
Boogie to New York.

Poem Of Thanks To Vasily Kandinsky –
Synaesthetic Spaceman

Even Kandinsky's name is strange
You have to be strangely read
To take Kandinsky to bed
His art is mystical and spiritual
This great inventor of the abstract
Through musical colours and forms
His new art created a storm

He draws on the occult
Multi sensory demands
Colour and sense theory
Though nature still has command
Objective, subjective, abstracted, lyrical
All these contents combine
To take you out of your mind

He and we owe it all
To Wagner's Lohengrin
Monet's Haystacks (uniquely perceived)
Arnold Schonberg. And Madam
Helena Petrovna Blavatsky
They all gave Kandinsky a call
Through 'The Great Gate of Kiev'
He invited us to the imaginary
Cosmic, abstract, geometric ball.

Helpful note: Can your ear be your eye?

Thoughts On Klee

Intelligent child etching his 'Inventions'

Stirring his sons feed with the end of his paintbrush
Lily is giving piano lessons
He, thinking of Tunisian colour codes:

Bern
Berlin
Blue riders
Bauhaus:
(Bern)

:Teaching Bauhaus language
Contemplates the 'dividual' and individual opposites

Visual music leads the line for a walk
Playing the violin, he composes with his thinking eye
Tablets of ancient harmony

Klee is his own poet
He has no need of me
He has entered the residential gardens and the torrid zones
Then left them for the main way and byways
Long before the world woke up.

Chagall

Russian memories combine with the joys of Paris
His secret soul recreates King David and floating imaginary
worlds of passion, expression and love
Creatures with invisible wings
Rotate mysteriously in his magical canvases
Above the cities and villages of his life

For these works are a celebration of life
All things simple become endowed with a spirit of wonder
His brush like wand puts us under a spell
We float into his dreams
All his works are windows to his soul
A journey of souls, carried by animal spirits to heavenly
bodies.
His subjects glow like stain glass
    Lovers embrace in space
    Stain glass blue, red and yellow
    Bouquets of blossoms fill the night skies
    Couples embrace on their wedding day
    Their feet do not touch the ground
    And their heads are in the stars

Chagall smiles on his works
Watched by his children, as the Alps Maritimes look back at
him
A true painter of the imagination
His sun will never go out.

Salvador Dali – An Imagination

Dali Dali Dali
Salvador Dali
Bound forever to Portlligat
An elite mind anchored to Catalonian soil
Exquisite family portraits contradict
Aristocratic anarchistic antics. The
Art student extraordinar, expelled –
To Picasso extends a complimentary hand
Experiments with Cubism, oil and sand

Not expressionistic
Not humanitarian, particularly
More visual prankster intent to shock surprise
An initial sadistic intelligence with a taste for the severe
Scholar of the psyche, nightmares and fear
Admirer of Freud and Vermeer

Tormented frustration, paranoiac images
Contortions of civil disasters
Fuel a contrived personal madness of liquid desires.
Time dissolves under his brush
His art a pathway to surrealism
Haunted by the dead shadow of his unseen brother
He enters the Surrealist group's inner circle
Sidesteps into avant-garde film
Dali becomes surrealism, a sensitivity soft and hard
(From Spain to France)
Is surrealism
To the ends of his moustache
Kissing the streets of America
Now a cult figure
The ultimate psychedelic walking dream

A one man street procession
The unconscious made real
In another land
Everywhere you turn
A mindscape burns

Strange fallings of classical sculptures
Rain from his head
Like a pharaoh everything he creates turns to gold
The Dalinian critical method pre-empts
His mature style
Childhood memories, reflections, sexual connections
Evoke associations, biomorphisms bizarre
Hallucinations of a hyper reality transpire

Gala enters the surrealist court
They are one, the centre of his art
The unique Dali's
(Christ of St John of the Cross, a masterpiece)
The religious super nature works
Nuclear energy, space, atomic Madonna's
Optics, illusions, stereoscopic perspectives
Hand photogenic techniques
His genius speaks
His world is complete

When Gala leaves
For thirty years a productive recluse
He follows her (closing his books of printed alchemy)
The king to his queen, the spiritual Dali
Leaving a strange testimony of his existence
Visual essence of Spanish castle hermitic years
Sacred imagery christens modern technology
A transmission of extra-terrestrial thoughts

Religious mysticism sold and bought.

Sir Howard Hodgkin

A real painter
An artist with a brave heart
An expressionistic Englishman
A great rarity
He has made his mark
Worthy of a knighthood
His paintings are just right
Stunning, so good
Hymns to life
Alone in his studio – a man apart
Well travelled and loved for himself and his art.

Famous friends depicted in their interiors
Paintings full of the sunlight of India and Venetian hotel
rooms
England in full bloom

His art is sumptuous velvet colours and dark textures
from nature's realm.
His paintings are silently singing the songs of the land,
the sun and the rain.

A passion for landscape
Look - that one of 'Scotland' (1995)
Just brilliant
Deeply aglow.
'Gardening' that's an early cracker
'Red Bermudas'
'Waking up in Naples'
'Then there's 'From the House of Bhupen Khakhar'
Oh yes, what about 'Venetian Glass'
The mystery of 'Snapshot'

And 'After Degas' – what an absolute gem
The green against the amber
I'd love any one of them!

His strength is that he makes art
By the simplest mans
Memories of passion, beauty serene
Transformed to heroic status
Visions of desires and dreams

His subject matter of majestic images
'Dark Moon', 'Passion' and 'Egyptian Night'
His titles are poetry in their own right
None but the brave deserve to view his works
An artist who has enriched the pleasure of sight.

Damien Hirst

Minus, dots, spots and rotating art
Hirst
I find
His work reminds
Of death life and birth
The poems of Dylan Thomas
But worse
With a large helping of science
Glass storage jars, bottles, flies
Dead meat
Cows, shark and sheep
Sometimes whole, sometimes divided
Very obvious, stunning deep –
Also unnerving
More dark than light
Not a sunflower in sight
Brit /Art sensation
Unhinged, a nightmare encased
But you know it looks right
With patience, planning and a good team
He eventually realises his 'dream'
A master of scale and space
Combines conceptual, installation, sculpture and place
More an idea
That hangs in the mind
This is his real strength
I find.

John Constable RA
Well Done John

Constable was revolutionary in his time
And not particularly liked
Always on the bottom line
Landscape painting was not
Considered so fine
As portrait nor historical no
Having to take third place
And keep face
At the Royal Academy

But he loved his wife
In the end it all turned out alright
For him
As landscape art was accepted as a science.

There is a great deal of emotion in his studies
Don't forget his stunning oil on paper sketches
Far superior to his lectures.

When caught with a fresh eye
'The Haywain' is a bloody good painting.